The Story of Money

by Betsy Maestro

ILLUSTRATED BY GIULIO MAESTRO

CLARION BOOKS
NEW YORK

The pictures of paper money and coins in this book are
approximately actual size, except where labeled otherwise.

(actual size)

This Greek coin, shown larger on the title page,
is from the city of Syracuse on the island of Sicily
(now part of Italy). It dates from about 400 B.C.

Clarion Books
a Houghton Mifflin Company imprint
215 Park Avenue South, New York, NY 10003
Text copyright © 1993 by Betsy Maestro
Illustrations copyright © 1993 by Giulio Maestro

Printed in the U.S.A.

Library of Congress Cataloging-in-Publication Data
Maestro, Betsy.
The story of money / by Betsy Maestro ; illustrated by Giulio
Maestro.
p. cm.
Summary: A history of money, beginning with the barter system in
ancient times, to the first use of coins and paper money, to the
development of modern monetary systems.
ISBN 0-395-56242-2
1. Money—History—Juvenile literature. 2. Money—United States—
History—Juvenile literature. [1. Money—History.] I. Maestro,
Giulio, ill. II. Title.
HG221.5.M25 1993   91-24997
332.4—dc20   CIP   AC

HOR 10 9 8 7 6 5 4 3 2 1

A long time ago, there was no such thing as money. The first humans had simple needs. They ate whatever they could find or catch. They wore the skins of the animals they killed for food. They lived in small groups in caves or in shelters they made themselves. Each family group depended only on itself for survival. Early humans had no need for money. There was no place to spend it— they had no stores where they could buy the things they needed.

Over thousands of years, the human way of life changed. As the numbers of people grew larger, more food was needed. In their search for food, family groups moved from place to place—to a big river far away to fish or to the forest to hunt small animals. Sometimes they traveled great distances, following herds of large game. Often they met other, unfamiliar groups of people along the way. After a while, fear of these strangers turned to interest and then to trust. In time, these different groups began to trade with one another.

The people in one group might trade some of their fish for small animal skins offered by the others. Any object could be exchanged for any other object if the two traders agreed. Pretty shells might be swapped for bright feathers. Trade, or barter, made it easier for people to get the things they wanted and needed. People began to travel long distances to meet and trade with one another.

Slowly, over more thousands of years, changes in climate and in plants and animals caused the human way of life to change again. The earth grew warmer. As many large game animals died out, hunting became more difficult. People began to live in small settlements and to look for new ways to get food. About ten thousand years ago, people began to farm the land. They learned to grow many of the plants that they used for food. They learned how to keep and raise animals on their farms. Most people settled in areas that had fertile, rich soil and a good supply of fresh water. Settlements grew into small towns and then larger ones.

Farms could produce enough food for many people. Not everyone had to spend time growing food. People had time to learn new skills—to specialize in other jobs. Herders raised meat animals for butchers to kill and prepare for eating. Farmers raised grain for millers to grind into flour for bakers to make into bread. Potters made the utensils to store and cook this food. Weavers, carpenters, boat builders, and metalsmiths could be found in most big towns.

Farmers and craftspeople could not use everything they grew or made. They began to sell what they could not use themselves—the extra, or surplus. On market day, people came from miles around to buy and sell goods. The marketplace in the center of town was a busy and very important place. Here, a goat might be traded for tools. A sack of grain could be swapped for a few baskets, woven cloth for a loaf of bread. Sometimes, a worker would trade a job for goods. A carpenter might fix a roof in exchange for materials like wood or nails. An artist could pay for food and lodging with a carving or painting.

No money changed hands in the marketplace. All the buying and selling was in the form of barter. By trading, people were able to get the things they wanted and needed. Goods and supplies not available locally were often brought from far away. Merchants traveled long distances by boat or on pack animals to bring back items made or grown in other places.

Most of the time this system of trade worked well. But sometimes, there were problems. Barter could work only when each trader wanted what the other had, and when both could agree on what made a fair trade. It could be difficult to work out an equal exchange when the items to be traded were very different from each other. The traders had to come to an agreement as to how many rugs might equal one cow or how many eggs would be exchanged for a loaf of bread.

To make trading easier, people began to use certain objects as money. Anything could be used as money if people agreed on its value and accepted it in trade for goods or labor. In many parts of the world, salt was used as money. Salt was valuable to people because they needed it to preserve and flavor food. It was also valuable because it was hard to find. Because it had great worth, people would accept salt as money.

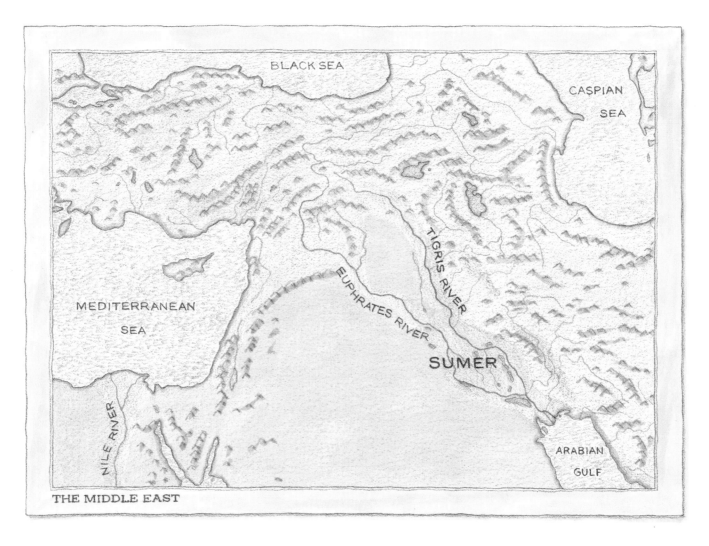

THE MIDDLE EAST

Many other objects were also used as money. Tea leaves, shells, feathers, animal teeth, tobacco, and blankets were some of the items used at times around the world. In ancient Sumer, a civilization that flourished about five thousand years ago in what is now the Middle East, barley was used as money. Workers received barley in payment for their labor. The barley could then be used to buy goods.

barley

barley grains

Although barley and salt and other objects were valuable, they were not always convenient to use. Salt could melt in the rain. Blankets were hard to carry. Feathers could blow away in the wind. Little metal balls used in some places often rolled away as they were counted.

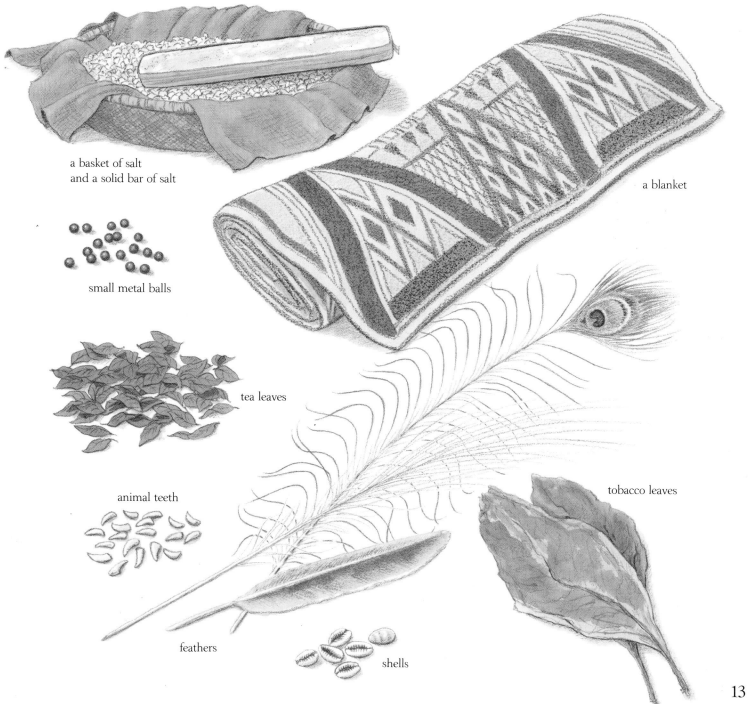

a basket of salt
and a solid bar of salt

small metal balls

a blanket

tea leaves

animal teeth

tobacco leaves

feathers

shells

Sumerian merchants sometimes traveled great distances to trade. Barley was hard to handle in large amounts and it sometimes spoiled on the journey. The merchants looked for a new medium of exchange. They needed something that was easy to handle and carry, something that wouldn't spoil or be damaged easily, and something that people everywhere would accept in trade. They began to use silver as money. Silver was a precious metal that was hard to find and so was very valuable. Everybody wanted it.

The Sumerians melted the silver and formed it into small bars. Each was stamped with its exact weight, which let people know how much silver they were getting or giving in return for goods or labor. The Sumerians had invented the world's first metal money.

The Sumerians invented the wheel and the sailboat, which made it possible to transport goods for trade farther than before. They sent grain and cloth to faraway lands in exchange for stone, wood, and metals they did not have at home. Trading brought about more than an exchange of goods. It also brought an exchange of ideas. The idea of money made from a precious metal spread from Sumer to all of its trading partners. More countries began to use silver in trade.

Lydian lion's head coins

About twenty-seven hundred years ago, coins were first used as the official money of a government. In 640 B.C., the ancient kingdom of Lydia, a land located in what is now Turkey, created a system of money. Each Lydian coin was guaranteed to be of an exact weight and purity. The coins were made of a mixture of gold and silver called electrum. These lumpy, bean-shaped coins were stamped with a lion's head—the mark of the king of Lydia. The people trusted the king, so they trusted the new money. They would accept the coins in trade for their goods and services.

(actual size)

Lion and bull coin (much larger than actual size)

Roman elephant coin (smaller than actual size)

Phoenician (Lebanese) chariot coin

Roman horse's head coin

Olbian (Russian) dolphin coin

Greek turtle coin

Chinese square hole coin

Coins were very easy to use as money. They were popular with the people. In time, the use of coins as official money was adopted by other governments. The ancient empires of Greece and Persia, and later Rome, all developed systems of coinage. Pictures of great leaders were often stamped on the faces of these coins. The use of coins spread throughout the world. Coins were made in many shapes and sizes. Most were round, but some were shaped like shells and animals. Others were ring-like, with holes in the middle. The coins were made of many metals—silver and gold, copper and bronze.

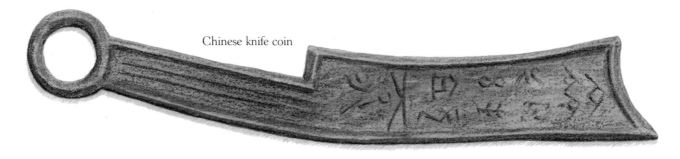

Chinese knife coin

Roman portrait coin

Etruscan (Italian)
seahorse coin

Chinese shell coin

Greek portrait coin

Mauryan (Indian)
coins

Ancient British coin

Egyptian coin

Even though money was now being used in trade in most of Europe, Asia, and the Middle East, the barter system did not disappear. In many places, people continued to trade item for item or to use valuable objects as money. This is true in some places even today.

Celtic (Belgian)
horse coin

Pakistani coin

Chinese
spade coin

Celtic (French)
portrait coin

Babylonian (Iraqi)
lion coin

Roman
Pegasus coin

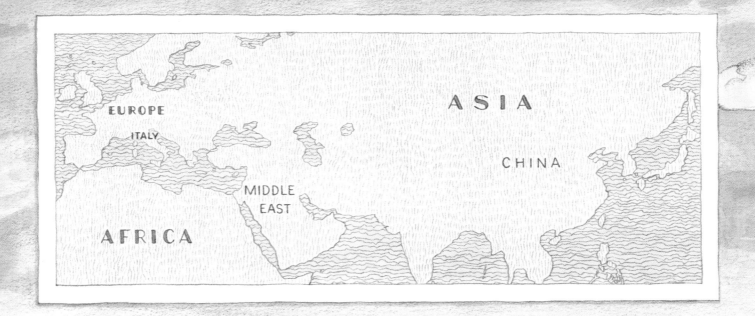

Toward the end of the Middle Ages, the adventurer Marco Polo traveled to China. When he returned to Italy in the year 1295, he brought news of some very interesting Chinese inventions. One of these ideas was considered very strange—money made of paper! The Chinese had been using paper money for hundreds of years before news of it reached Europe.

The Chinese did not have a good supply of the metals needed to make coins. So they invented a system of money in which no metal was used. Much earlier, the Chinese had invented both paper and a printing process. They used these inventions to create their new money—money printed on paper. Each paper note was guaranteed by the government to have a certain value.

The Chinese government ordered the new paper money to be used everywhere in China. The government was very strong, so people obeyed the order to use the new money. When the people saw that they could buy whatever they wanted with the paper money, they came to trust it. They trusted it because it worked. The new paper money worked because the Chinese government was powerful enough to guarantee its worth.

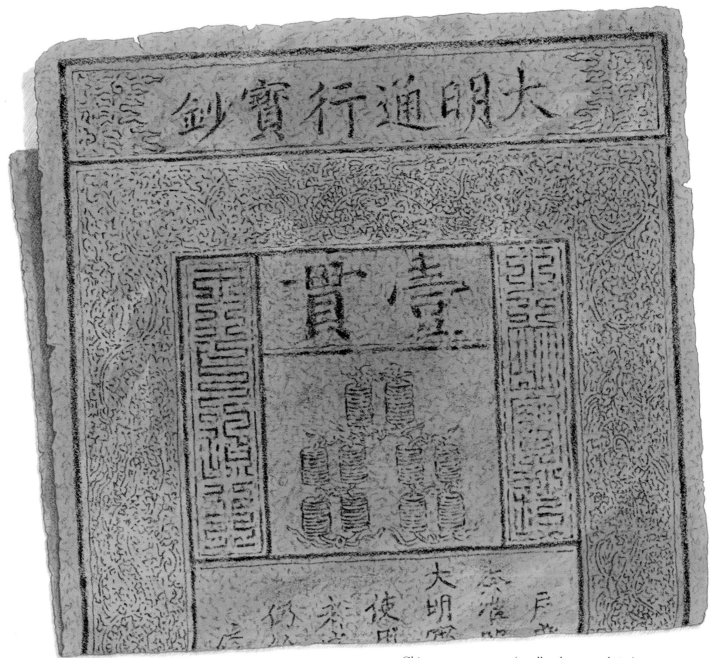

Chinese paper money (smaller than actual size)

Europeans thought that the idea of paper money was interesting, but they were not ready to begin using it themselves. Europe in the Middle Ages was made up of many small kingdoms and states that were constantly at war with one another. It was a time of disorder and change. People did not have confidence in their governments. They would not trust paper money made by those governments. The people felt safer using the coins they were used to. Gold and silver were precious metals that would always have value even if governments changed. Hundreds of years would pass before the people of Europe would begin to use paper money. In 1661, Sweden became the first European country to print money made of paper.

Swedish paper money
(smaller than actual size)

A Spanish
"piece of eight"

"bits"

By the early 1500s, sailing ships had been improved, making long ocean voyages possible. New sea routes were discovered. Europeans could now sail to the Far East and to the New World. In the Americas, Spanish conquerors seized large deposits of gold and silver which they mined and made into crude or rough coins. Spain became the richest and most powerful country in the world.

A coin minted at the silver mountain mines of Potosí (South America), in operation between 1545 and 1800.

Spanish coins and "bits" used
by some Caribbean islands

St. Vincent

St. Lucia

St. Martin

Dominica

Trinidad & Tobago

Having big ships at sea increased trade between nations. Countries would often trade in goods—barter on a grand scale. Large amounts of money also moved from country to country as payment for goods. Millions of Spanish silver coins, called "pieces of eight," were sent all over the globe. There were so many of these "Spanish dollars" that many countries adopted them as their own official money. The coins were changed in some way—cut or stamped—to show that they were now the currency of another country. To make change, the pieces of eight could be cut into smaller pieces, or "bits." Until 1850, the Spanish dollar was the coin most widely used throughout the world.

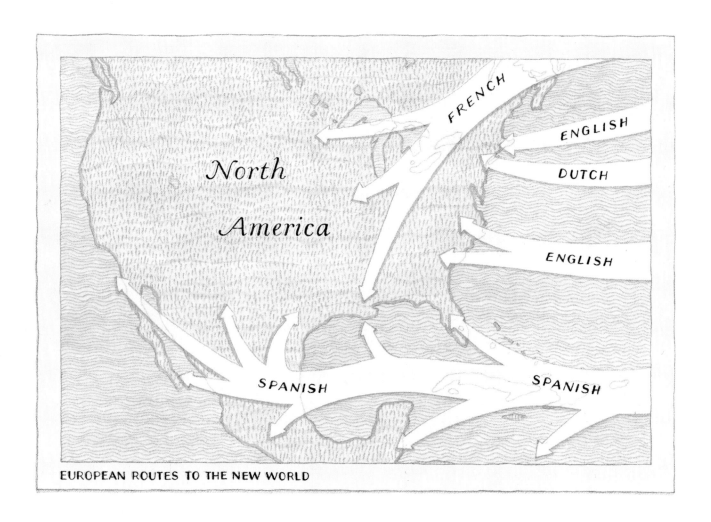

EUROPEAN ROUTES TO THE NEW WORLD

By 1650, France, England, and Holland had joined Spain in establishing colonies in the New World. Ships from these countries arrived often in colonial ports, and money from all four countries circulated freely throughout the colonies. The early settlers of North America traded fish, furs, and lumber for European goods or money.

French colony coin   English coin   Dutch coin   Spanish doubloon

26

European coins could then be used to purchase colonial goods. Coins, however, were not the only acceptable form of payment in the colonies. Settlers frequently paid their bills and taxes with other objects—corn, tobacco, fish, wheat, and even nails. Wampum was also used as money by the colonists. This Native American money was made of shell beads strung together as belts, bracelets, and necklaces. The colonists first accepted wampum in trade with the native people. In time, because coins were often in short supply, the colonists began to make and use wampum themselves.

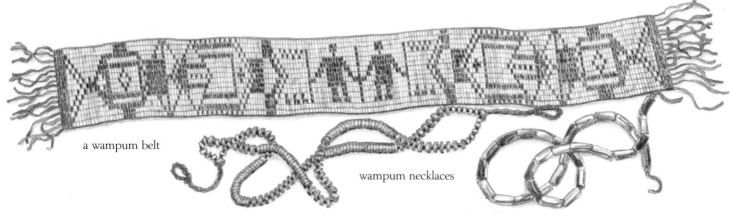

a wampum belt

wampum necklaces

Massachusetts
Pine Tree shilling

One of the first coins to be made, or minted, in colonial America was known as a Pine Tree shilling, because a pine tree was stamped on one side. These silver coins were made in Boston, Massachusetts, in 1652. After the American Revolution in 1776, all the colonies began to make their own money—coins and paper bills. With currency from thirteen different colonies added to the foreign money in circulation, trading became confusing and difficult.

Pennsylvania

Maryland

Connecticut

New Jersey

New York

Vermont

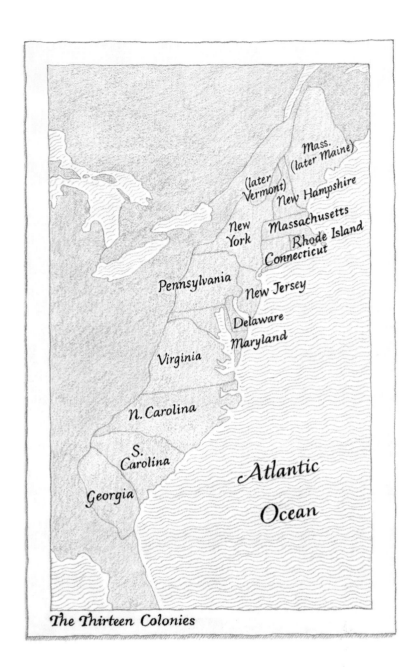

The Thirteen Colonies

1787 "Fugio" cent

The Continental Congress established a single, official currency for all the colonies to use. In 1787, the first coin was minted in New Haven, Connecticut. It was a copper cent, stamped with the words WE ARE ONE and MIND YOUR BUSINESS. Thirteen linked circles decorated this coin, symbolizing the thirteen colonies that had joined together in the fight for independence from Great Britain.

In 1790, the Constitution was ratified and the United States of America officially became a country. The new Congress agreed on a money system that would become law and would be used by all the states. This new system would have a dollar as the basic unit and would use both gold and silver in the coins.

A mint was opened in Philadelphia in 1792 to make gold, silver, and copper coins. There was not enough precious metal available to make all the new coins that the country needed, so ordinary citizens contributed candlesticks, jewelry, and other valuable objects to be melted down. There is a story that the first coins minted were made from George Washington's own family silver. No one knows if this is true. Although foreign coins were ordered to be melted down as well, Americans continued to use them for many years.

The first Philadelphia Mint

The Denver Mint

The Philadelphia Mint made all the coins used in the United States until 1838. Six other mints were opened over the years to keep up with the country's need for coinage. Today, only the mints at Philadelphia and Denver still make coins. The new Philadelphia Mint is the largest in the world. When it is not busy making United States coins, it mints coins for other nations.

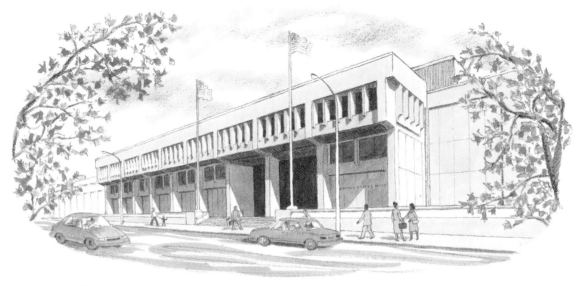

The new Philadelphia Mint

Shiny new "blanks"

A special design is created for each new coin. Liquid metal is poured into molds to make bars, or "ingots." Machines with heavy rollers press the ingots to make thin sheets of metal. After steel presses punch out the blank coin shapes, the design is stamped, or "struck," onto each "blank." All United States coins have two sayings stamped on them: E PLURIBUS UNUM (Latin for "out of many, one"), and IN GOD WE TRUST.

United States paper money is printed at the Bureau of Engraving and Printing in Washington, D.C. This is a branch of the United States Mint that also prints postage stamps, savings bonds, and government checks. Paper money is printed on large sheets of special paper made from a blend of cotton and linen. The ink that is used is mixed from a secret formula. As many as thirty-two bills can be printed on each sheet. Then they are cut out, pressed, starched, and wrapped in bundles. Each bill has its own serial number for identification.

Several times a month, new paper money and new coins are delivered to twelve special banks around the country. These banks send the new money to smaller banks which put it into circulation. The government keeps a careful count of how much money is made and put into use. When paper money gets too old or worn, or when it is damaged, it is taken out of use and burned. New bills are printed to replace it. Coins that become too old and worn are melted down and made into new coins.

Old money being burned

Most countries make their own money. All money is made very carefully to ensure that bills and coins of the same amount are always exactly the same in size, weight, and appearance. Each country has its own special ink and paper and its own secret process for coining and printing official money. It is impossible for anyone to produce fake or counterfeit money that is exactly like the real thing. It is against the law in all countries to make copies of official money.

Almost every country has its own official currency. There are about one hundred forty different currencies in use today. French francs, German marks, Japanese yen, Mexican pesos, Chinese yuan, Swedish kronor, and English pounds are just a few.

Mexico

Germany

France

Japan

England

37

The money systems in use today were adopted by most countries in the late 1800s. All include both paper money and metal coins. At first, coins were made only from precious metals. Today, most coins are made from mixtures of cheaper metals that are more plentiful in the world.

Over time, paper money has replaced coins in importance. All over the world, people accept paper money. When it was first used, it was like a written promise of payment. If people wanted to, they could exchange their paper money for gold or silver stored by the government. This is no longer true. Although many governments still store large quantities of these metals, there is not enough to exchange for all the paper money in use today. But people do not worry about the value of their paper money. All over the world, people have come to value paper money for itself.

Today, ideas about money are pretty much the same all over the world. People must have money to survive. They work at jobs, trading their labor for the money they need to pay for the goods and services that make their lives comfortable. The marketplace has grown to include the whole world. Modern transportation has made it possible for all countries of the world to ship and receive goods from abroad. Nations trade with one another by exchanging goods: machinery for sugar, oil for grain—goods are traded in huge quantities in the world market. Countries also exchange currencies. There are official rates of exchange that let people know just how many yen, marks, or pesos equal one dollar, one franc, or one krona. These exchange rates can change from day to day.

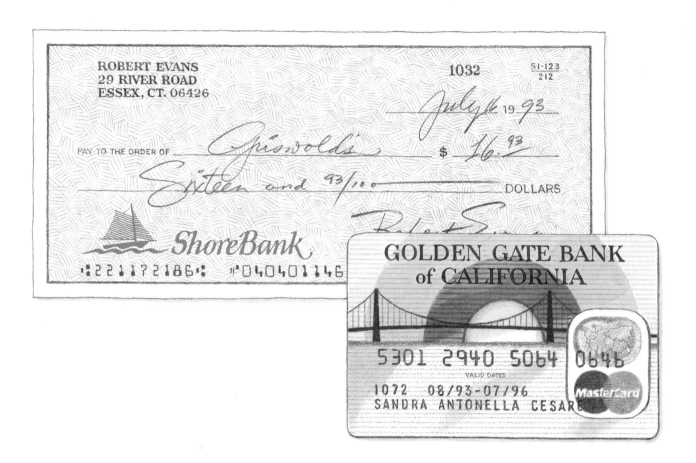

In recent years, people have begun to use a system of cashless money. One very popular kind of cashless money is called a check. People write checks every day to pay their bills and to purchase goods. The company or the merchant who is owed the money will then be paid by the check-writer's bank. Credit cards are another kind of cashless money. People use credit cards because they are easy to use and allow people to buy now and pay later.

The world has entered an electronic age and the latest form of cashless money is information stored in bank computers. People can have their paychecks electronically added to their bank accounts. Their bills can then be paid directly by the bank using advanced communication systems. No actual money changes hands. Everything is recorded by computer. Banks can transfer this electronic money all over the world in minutes. Home computers allow people to do their banking without leaving their houses.

Automated teller machines, located outside banks and in stores, let people do their banking even when banks are closed. In the future, there will be other kinds of electronic cashless money.

When people think of money, they often think of cash—the paper money and coins they are most familiar with. But money can be anything that people use to exchange for goods and services. It can be anything from salt to electronic cards. Money is a tool that has changed as the world has changed. Now it is changing again. No one knows for sure what the money of the future will be.

Additional Information About Money

SOME UNUSUAL MONEY

Native Americans used money before European settlers arrived. In the Pacific Northwest, a number of coastal tribes used large shield-like copper plates as money. The plates could be as large as three feet high. The copper was beaten by hand and had animal faces carved on it. One plate could be worth more than five thousand blankets.

Feather money was used by some Pacific Islanders. Small feathers were glued and tied together to form coils up to thirty feet long. Yap Islanders used the world's heaviest money. The round stones with holes in the middle were as large as twelve feet across. Some of this money is still exchanged on ceremonial occasions.

In Ethiopia, salt was used as money until World War II. Black salt, dug out of the mountains, was made into slabs or bars. Coins were accepted only in the larger towns. Salt is an essential item in hot climates and its use as money lasted for centuries.

Large bracelet-like objects called manillas were often used in European trade with West Africa in the 1500s and 1600s. When the Portuguese first came to Africa to trade, they discovered that many tribal groups had a liking for horseshoe-shaped metal objects. They then made and shipped thousands of similar metal bracelets to Africa where they traded them for slaves. Manillas were made in many sizes, of a lead and copper mixture which produced a much-valued ringing sound. They were used in Nigeria until 1948.

Platmynt, or plate money, was minted in Sweden between 1644 and 1809. These coins were the largest ever circulated. The ten-Daler plate was the biggest and weighed about forty-three pounds.

Many different kinds of money were made and circulated in the American colonies. Tobacco leaves, tied in bundles, were the official currency of Virginia and Maryland during the 1600s and 1700s. Around 1685, the French colonies in Canada printed money in the form of playing cards, complete with four suits.

MORE ABOUT MONEY

Banking began during the Middle Ages as a way to help merchants pay for trading activities. Modern commercial banking began in Italy in the fourteenth century. The word *bank* comes from the Italian word *banca*, which means the counter or bench where money was laid out.

The use of the word *dollar* can be traced back to a large silver Tyrolian or Austrian coin. This coin, minted around 1518 in Joachimsthal, Bohemia, soon became known as a Joachimsthaler. The name was shortened to thaler, and then in English became dollar. Later, during the height of the Spanish Empire, a coin worth eight reales was circulated throughout the world. It became known as a Spanish dollar. The word was adopted in many places and is still used today.

During World War II, many countries experienced a shortage of copper, which was used in the manufacture of shell casings. Other metals like iron, aluminum, and zinc were substituted in the making of coins.

The modern currencies of China and Japan developed from the introduction of silver dollars used in trading with Europeans in the 1500s. The dollars were called "round coins," which in Chinese is *yuan* and in Japanese is *yen*. The Chinese yuan and the Japanese yen are the official monetary units today.

Numismatics is the collecting and studying of coins. Many people collect coins as a hobby, while others study them because of their important part in world history. Many museums have large collections of interesting coins from all over the world. Ancient coins have been uncovered by archeologists. Many coin collectors are interested in more modern coinage.

MORE ABOUT AMERICAN MONEY

Most of America's gold—billions of dollars' worth—is stored at Fort Knox, Kentucky. The gold ingots, or bars, are kept in a granite block building inside steel and concrete vaults. The United States Gold Bullion Depository stands on the corner of Gold Vault Drive and Bullion Boulevard. It is bomb-proof and is protected by well-armed security guards and many alarm systems. United States silver is stored in a depository in West Point, New York.

An eagle named Peter lived at the first United States Mint in Philadelphia. He flew around the city during the day and at night returned to the mint to roost. He was said to have been the model for the eagle on the silver dollars circulated from 1836 to 1839. After he died of an injury, he was stuffed and mounted, and he is now on display in the lobby of the present Philadelphia Mint.

The United States dollar has been the same size since 1929. It is 2.61 inches high, 6.14 inches wide, and .0043 inches thick. It takes 233 bills stacked together to equal one inch.

Indian Head, or Buffalo, nickels were circulated between 1913 and 1938. The coin had a buffalo on one side and a portrait of a Native American on the other. It was designed to honor both the buffalo and Native Americans, which represented a vanishing way of life. Artist James Fraser created the portrait from his drawings of three Native Americans. The buffalo Fraser used as his model lived in the Central Park Zoo in New York City.

In 1979, a dollar coin with a portrait of Susan B. Anthony was minted. Susan B. Anthony was a leader in the movement to gain voting rights for women in the late 1800s. This new, smaller dollar was expected to be popular and reduce the demand for paper dollars. Instead, people did not like using the new coin, as they often confused it with a quarter. Millions were minted but only a small number ever circulated. Over 400 million of these dollar coins had to be put into storage.

There are five coins and six bills in common everyday use in the United States. They all have portraits of presidents or other important statesmen on the front, and buildings, seals, or symbols on the reverse.

Coin or Bill	Front	Reverse
Penny or one cent	Abraham Lincoln	Lincoln Memorial
Nickel or five cents	Thomas Jefferson	Monticello
Dime or ten cents	Franklin D. Roosevelt	Liberty torch, oak & olive branches
Quarter or twenty-five cents	George Washington	Eagle, arrows, & olive branch
Half dollar or fifty cents	John F. Kennedy	Eagle & shield
One-dollar bill	George Washington	Great Seal of the U.S.
Five-dollar bill	Abraham Lincoln	Lincoln Memorial
Ten-dollar bill	Alexander Hamilton	U.S. Treasury Building
Twenty-dollar bill	Andrew Jackson	The White House
Fifty-dollar bill	Ulysses S. Grant	U.S. Capitol Building
One-hundred-dollar bill	Benjamin Franklin	Independence Hall

SOME MONEY OF OTHER COUNTRIES

Brazil: New Cruzado

Canada: Dollar

China: Yuan

Czechoslovakia: Koruna

Ecuador: Sucre

Ethiopia: Birr

Finland: Markka

France: Franc

The Gambia: Dalasi

Germany: Mark

Greece: Drachma

India: Rupee

Indonesia: Rupiah

Israel: Shekel

Italy: Lira

Japan: Yen

Jordan: Dinar

Laos: New Kip

Mexico: Peso

Mongolia: Tugrik

Morocco: Dirham

Netherlands: Guilder

Nicaragua: Cordoba

Nigeria: Naira

Poland: Zloty

Saudi Arabia: Riyal

Spain: Peseta

Sweden: Krona

Thailand: Baht

United Kingdom: Pound

Venezuela: Bolivar

Zambia: Kwacha